ISBN 0-345-29448-3

Manufactured in the United States of America

First Edition: May 1971

9 8 7 6 5 4 3

Symbols of Tyranny
Introduction by Alan Wykes

The bright colours and ornate designs which decorate these pages have behind them a history of horror. The oppression and destruction of six million Jews is alone a testimony to that horror. But it is only a segment of it. The régime that afflicted Germany from 1933 to 1945 – its chief proponent, Adolf Hitler, had promised that this, the Third Reich, would last for a thousand years – concentrated into its short span a whole dark age that could vie with anything in the longer Dark Ages of the history books. The merciless barbarism of medieval rulers who struck at philosophies that challenged their authority was well matched by the atrocities of Belsen, Dachau and Buchenwald.

But one did not have to be Jewish to end up in those grim places. One of the directives issued by Göebbels, the Nazi Propaganda Minister, after a conference on the morning of 31st July 1940 said:

'A Potsdam priest is reported to have said in a sermon: "Lord, have mercy upon our young people who go through life without a purpose". If this report is correct Herr Guttere [one of Goebbels' minions] is to make it clear to that priest, beyond any possibility of doubt, that in the event of a repetition he will find himself in a concentration camp.'

The young people in Germany from 1933 onward had in fact a very real purpose: to fulfil the establishment of despotism. And they followed it in the regalia of the Hitler Youth – one of many uniforms in which Hitler's followers, willingly or by coercion, strutted upon the stage of evil.

Regalia, in its strict sense, means the insignia of royalty – the crown, orb, sceptre and other appurtenances of the sovereign. But like many another word it has come to be used where it fits conveniently; and it has been borrowed by church, civic, military and Masonic fraternities to describe the uniforms and ornaments that make them recognizable to outsiders and, within their own fraternity, display their degrees of authority and achievement.

This book displays the regalia adopted by a group of people whose dedicated purpose in life was tyranny. Being German and having a language lacking the conveniences of simplicity, their nomenclature was complex: *Nationalsozialistische Deutsche Arbeiterpartei* – National Socialist German Workers' Party. For convenient abbreviation's sake they abstracted two pairs of letters, joined them, and made *Nazi,* which at least was easier to say and took less time in the saying.

The symbol most readily associated with the Nazis is of course the swastika; and indeed it forms part of most of the emblems, uniforms and accoutrements shown here. There are still those who believe that the swastika was invented by Hitler, and to them a word of enlightenment must be offered.

The Swastika is almost as old as tyranny itself, though not originally – or indeed for centuries – particularly associated with that unpleasant characteristic. It is simply one of several kinds of cross, and the cross was an artifact of religious mysticism long before Christianity – indeed in prehistoric days. Two of the most familiar crosses are those known for convenience's sake as the Greek, which has four arms of equal length, and the Latin, which has one arm longer than the other three and is most readily recognized as the instrument of crucifixion. The swastika is an adaptation of the Greek cross with its arms extended at right (or sometimes left) angles to symbolize the movement of the sun. The word itself was originally Sanskrit and meant 'good luck', which is hardly what it came to mean under the Nazi régime.

Swastikas have been found in the pictorial records of religions all over the world – Egyptian, Greek, Chinese, Japanese, Amerindian, Persian. Invariably they were objects of veneration and tokens of propitiation and affection. Hitler, of course, has changed all that; but let no credit be given personally to him for changing the meaning. His mind was incapable of original thought and he merely carried on the use of the swastika from an earlier anti-Semitic organization in Germany called the *Hakenkreuzler* (hooked cross). The *Hakenkreuzler* chose it because in obliterating the Jewish Star of David from the walls of synagogues, which they frequently did, they needed to identify themselves by a more conspicuous graffito than a plain Greek cross. Hitler's sole contribution to the adaptation of the swastika as the Nazi symbol was to design the banner of red (for blood), white (for the purity of the Aryan race) and black (for the total eclipse of all non-Aryan races).

Of banners in general it may be said that 'Rally round the flag, lads' expresses their purpose completely. They were of course originally taken on to the battlefield as a convenient indication for a rallying point and bore devices, or were of some conspicuous colour, to ensure that friends and foes were not inextricably mixed — not an unlikely occurrence when everybody was wearing armour. In modern times they are wholly symbolic and decorative. Hitler combined the two purposes on occasions like the vast assemblies of Nazis at such gatherings as the Nuremberg Rallies, where thousands upon thousands of banners and similar samples of the creed's regalia — gonfalons, shields, hatchments, crests and the like — were marched through the streets, paraded in the arenas, and draped about buildings so that they were impressively inescapable and therefore aided the creed psychologically.

So far as the gorgeousness of their raiment was concerned the Italians always had the edge on the other Axis powers. It was positively Ruritanian. The Germans settled for the practical and sombre rather than the gorgeous. But no one could equal them in the width of the psychologically influential net they spread over civil, political, military and para-military branches of the organization. The Nazi Party was everywhere evident; and its protocol was distinguished by its insignia — witness the infinite variety shown here. You will find medals for varying degrees of valour and achievement, medallions to commemorate occasions such as games and rallies, weapons with subtle distinctions implied by the decoration of haft or blade, gorgets, tabs and lanyards to declare rank or regimental fervour. Everyone in any kind of official position, civil or military, was instantly recognizable through the descriptive language of regalia.

No one would claim that the language was the exclusive province of the Nazis, or indeed of Germany. Every country sophisticated enough to divide its people into classes and military or political organizations declares rank and privilege through dress and decoration. And it is obvious that armies find such a language necessary. Otherwise it would be impossible to distinguish leaders from followers, airmen from infantrymen, rewarded courage from mere participation.

The followers of Adolf Hitler had great difficulty in establishing themselves as an organization in any effective sense. Para-military organizations, including 'societies of discharged soldiers . . . and, generally speaking, associations of every description, whatever be the age of their members', were forbidden by Article 177 of the Versailles Treaty to 'instruct or exercise their members, or to allow them to be instructed or exercised, in the profession or use of arms'. Nothing was said in the Treaty about ideologies or the receptiveness to them of wavering minds; nor were uniforms and regalia as such proscribed. Indeed, had such a ban been considered it would have been insuperably difficult to define both words absolutely, the general principles of dress being what they are. Every ideology, however, encounters resistance from rival ideologies or the establishment or both. The German government of the early 1920s, the Weimar Republic, offered one core of resistance to Nazism. A much bitterer resistance came from the rival ideology of Communism ('Bolshevism' was the vogue word then). Their goal also was tyranny, but they sought to achieve it by a different route. As with all ideologies whose only certain way of gaining converts is to force their views on wavering minds, the rivalry between them resulted in physical violence. A natural corollary of such violence was a corps of strong-arm thugs to deal with it. To quote Hitler:

'The National Socialist Movement in Munich will in future ruthlessly prevent – if necessary by force – all meetings or lectures that are likely to distract the minds of our fellow countrymen.' (Munich, 4th January 1921). And again:

'Our motto shall be, "If you will not be a German, I will bash your skull in". For we are convinced that we cannot succeed without a struggle. We have to fight with ideas, but, if necessary, also with our fists.' (Munich, 7th November 1922).

The thugs were recruited from the *Freikorps,* ex-service men who were only too anxious in their bitterness to vent their spleen physically. They grew from a small group assigned to duties as Hitler's bodyguard into the formidable Storm Troops and they identified themselves as different from, and no doubt superior to, mere Party members by among other things belt buckles. That belt buckle was one of the earliest bits of Nazi regalia. Only the swastika armband, which served in the office of a uniform before the Party was able to afford such luxuries, was earlier. To have called this private army Storm Troops would only have ensured its disbandment under the treaty, so the euphemistic

'Gymnastic and Sports Division' was adopted as a title. Behind that title, which itself had a regalia of achievement in the field of athletics, grew an organization designed, according to the Party Proclamation dated 3rd August 1921, 'to serve as a means for bringing our youthful members together in a powerful organization for the purpose of utilizing their strength as an offensive force at the disposal of the movement'. In other words the German Army. And once established it proved far less difficult to promote its growth. It is astonishing how comparatively simple it is to recruit converts to a cause once its regalia has become familiar. Hitler, whose earliest official job in the Party had been that of Publicity Officer, knew this very well. For that reason he consistently used the swastika symbol in conjunction with the national emblem of Germany – the eagle.

The eagle had been adopted as a symbol of temporal power by Ptolemy of Egypt, Tarquin of Rome, Charlemagne, and Napoleon (whose regiments carried gilded eagles instead of banners). To Hitler's followers it meant the recovery of national greatness by way of Nazism. Stylized in design by Hitler's armaments minister Albert Speer (who was also an architect), it spread its huge wings over Party rallies and in miniature decorated the breasts of countless uniforms. Thus national glory was used as a justification for Nazi tyranny.

Hitler was from the first incapable of delegating authority, in small things as in great. (His refusal to accept the battle strategy of his generals was one of the causes of his military downfall.) The design of the smallest part of the most insignificant Party member's regalia was submitted to him for approval. Often that approval was given only after changes had been made; and often those changes were psychologically sound. He was well aware of the basic dichotomy behind man's wish to conform and at the same time to display evidence of uniqueness. Those *corps d'élite,* the Storm Troops (SA: *Sturm Abteilung*)and Blackshirts (SS: *Schutz Staffel*), had instantly recognizable regalia of their own which was as lauded as the belt buckle of the 'Gymnastic and Sports Division'. But the outstanding achievement of a mother who had borne eight or more children to serve the Nazi state also was recognized. Her fertility was rewarded by the gilt *Ehrenzeichen der Deutschen Mutter* (Cross of Honour of the German Mother). If she'd managed only six or seven children the cross was silver; and for a mere four or five, bronze. It didn't matter: the principle of achievement marked by a bit of regalia was the important thing.

Alone among the Nazi factions the Gestapo (another abstracted abbreviation from *Geheime Staatspolizei,* secret state police) needed no regalia to demonstrate its power, though its members often hid behind the uniforms or decorations of other factions. Officially it was a branch of the SS and the executives of its power wore the sinister black *Schutz Staffel* uniform on their terrifying visits to arrest suspects at dead of night. But though the SS were the inquisitorial functionaries the true Gestapo members were the anonymous spies who noted 'overheard' conversations, opened letters, tapped telephones, and passed on the scraps of information that accumulated in the dossiers of their all-powerful chief Heinrich Himmler, a man of colourless personality, and docile to the point of cringing subservience to his Führer and the 'ideals' of Nazism.

Curiously, it was the extrovert Hermann Göring who founded the Gestapo when he was Prime Minister of Prussia in 1933. But it was only the decorative side of any of his numerous offical positions that appealed to him. He collected the regalia of his offices for their own sake, to satisfy his infantile mania for dressing up. Anything secret and anonymous was useless to him. He kept his nominal power as founder and head of the Gestapo for a time but handed over the executive duties to Himmler, who was more interested in the symbols of the concentration camp and the gas chamber.

For those monstrous monuments to tyranny also had their regalia. The yellow Star of David ordered to be worn as a humiliation by the Jews in the earlier stages of the pogrom, and the distinguishing marks to differentiate those whose destinations were the gas chamber or the 'experimental' wards of Dachau or Buchenwald were the gruesome decorations of the fated. It is true that those kingdoms of death needed no regalia to express their horror. But it is just as true, and it must never be forgotten, that behind the festive note struck by the colourful pages of his book with their displays of uniforms and banners, their baubles, decorated sheaths, ribbons and awards, there lay the bloody shadows of extermination. These are the symbols of tyranny.

Deutsches Kreuz (German Cross). Awarded in two classes – gold and silver – it was intended to bridge the considerable gulf between the Iron Cross, First Class and the Knight's Cross

1 Dagger or hewer of the RAD – Reichsarbeitsdienst (German Labour Service).
Inscription: 'Work ennobles'. **2** Sports vest insignia of the RAD

Shop sign for official retailer of party badges and equipment

Insignia of Reserve, Old comrades, and Para-military organisations. 1 Leader's armband of the Reichskriegerbund (National Veterans Organisation). 2 Cap badge of the Kyffhaüserbund (Old Comrades Association for First World War Veterans). 3 Cap badge of the Landwacht, the auxiliary rural police (for translation of German terms see the list at the end of the book). 4 Badge of a Berlin group of the Ex-Servicemen's League. 5 and 6 Alternative cap badges of the Kyffhaüserbund. 7 Honours badge of the Stahlhelm. 8 Tenth anniversary badge of the NSDFB. 9 Armband badge of the Kyffhaüserbund. 10 Early cap badge of the Kyffhaüserbund

1 Political leader's armband. 2 SS. 3 NSDAP Party. 4 Hitler Youth. 5 Sport Leader,
SA Corps

Badge of Honour for the Dr Fritz Todt Prize. On the second anniversary of the death of Dr Fritz Todt, 8th February 1944, this award was instituted for inventions which furthered the war effort. It was awarded in three classes, denoted by gilt, silver, and black steel

Silver Warrant identity disc carried by all members of the Gestapo, giving the holder unlimited right of access, examination and arrest

Gestapo Warrant, reverse side

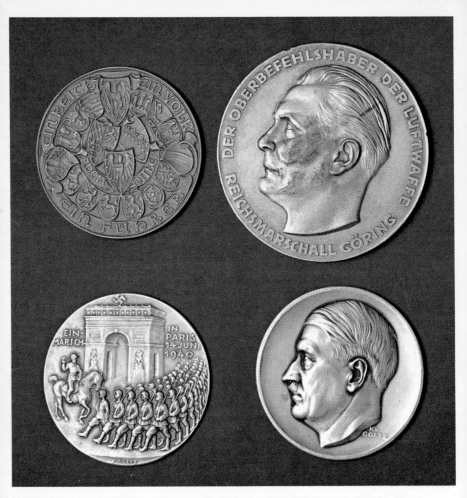

Commemorative medallions. *Top left:* Medallion of 'The Holy German Reich'. The inscription reads 'One Reich, One People, One Führer'. *Top right:* Medallion awarded for outstanding technical performance in the service of the Luftwaffe, showing the head of Reichsmarshal Göring. *Bottom left:* Medallion struck to commemorate the entry into France, 14th June 1940. The reverse reads 'The German Watch in France'. *Bottom right:* Adolf Hitler medallion

Reverse sides of the medals opposite

Hitler Jugend (Hitler Youth) insignia. 1 Sleeveband of the Landdienst (Land service) of the HJ. 2 Sleeve badge of the HJ Obergau Süd Schwaben. 3 Swastika armband worn by all ranks of the HJ. 4 HJ knife; Inscription: 'Blood and Honour'. 5 HJ sports vest badge

Nazi Red Cross dagger

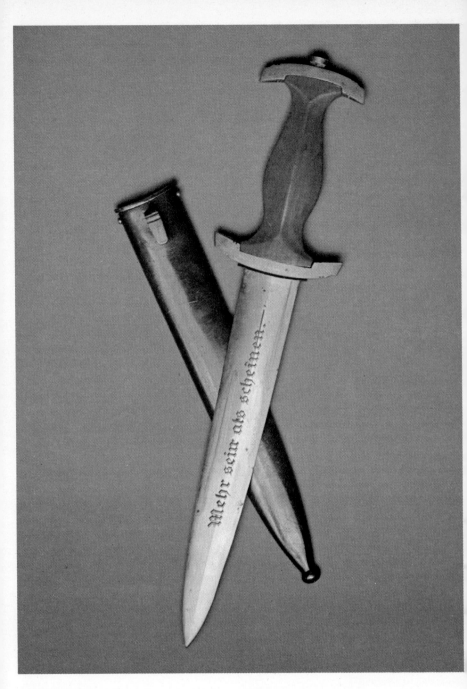

National Political Educational Institution dagger; Inscription: 'Be greater than you seem'

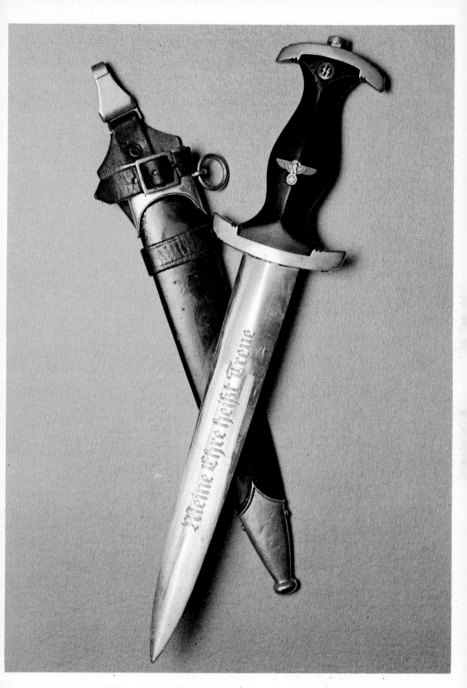

SS service dagger, 1933 pattern. Worn by all ranks in the Allgemeine SS who had served for three years as a candidate. Inscription: 'My honour is my pledge'

Comparison of 16th century hunting dagger and SS dagger

Service Dress tunic of a Hauptbereichsleiter (for table of equivalent ranks in other services see end of book). In the buttonhole is the War Merit Cross Second Class and on the left breast pocket the Iron Cross First Class of the First World War

Service dress tunic of a Hauptstürmführer of the 12th Stürm 78th Standarte of the SA Group Nordsee

Field tunic of a Rottenführer (corporal) in the 2nd SS Panzer Division.
The Waffenfarbe (Arm of Service colour) round the shoulder straps shows this to be the
tunic of an artilleryman; it is also clearly an army pattern tunic. Towards the end of
the war, because of the crippled German economy, the SS adopted more and more
items of army equipment as they could no longer rely on their own factories. On the
left collar patch is the SS rank insignia, and on the left sleeve, below the distinctive SS
pattern eagle, is the equivalent army rank insignia. On the lower left sleeve is the
divisional sleeveband, worn by most of the 38 SS divisions in the field by 1945

Uniform of a Hauptstürmführer (captain) in the Sicherheitsdienst (Security Service of the SS). Identical in cut to the black SS tunic, with open neck and turnback cuffs, it was introduced as a more practical and less obtrusive alternative to the black uniform. Because their duties were parallel in some aspects to those of a police unit, the SD wore police pattern shoulder straps with a black underlay. Here, the right collar patch shows that the wearer is attached to one of the three Hauptämter (Main Offices); the left collar patch denotes his SS rank. On the right sleeve can be seen the SS 'Old Fighter's Chevron'. This could be worn by anyone affiliated to the Nazi Party before January 1933, or by anyone who was a member of a Nazi organisation in Austria before that date. On the left sleeve is the SS pattern eagle and swastika, below it the distinctive badge of the SD. In the buttonhole is the Iron Cross, Second Class and on the left breast pocket the Iron Cross, First Class and the Deutschesreiterabzeichen (German Horseman's Badge); this was not a Nazi award, but it received official sanction from Hitler and could be worn with any Nazi uniform.

Selection of Waffen SS Items. 1 Shoulder strap of an SS Sturmscharführer (sergeant major). The blue piping denotes the medical branch of the Waffen SS. 2 Sleeveband of the 17th Panzer Division. 3 SS Deathshead cap badge worn by all ranks from 1936 to 1945. 4 Sleeveband of Panzer Grenadier Regiment No 10. 5 SS collar patch worn by all Germanic Waffen SS units. 6 SS collar patch; the left patch always showed rank insignia – in this case Rottenführer (Corporal). 7 Sleeveband of the 10th SS Panzer Division. 8 Sleeveband of the SS Gebirgsjager (Mountain Rifle) Regiment No 11

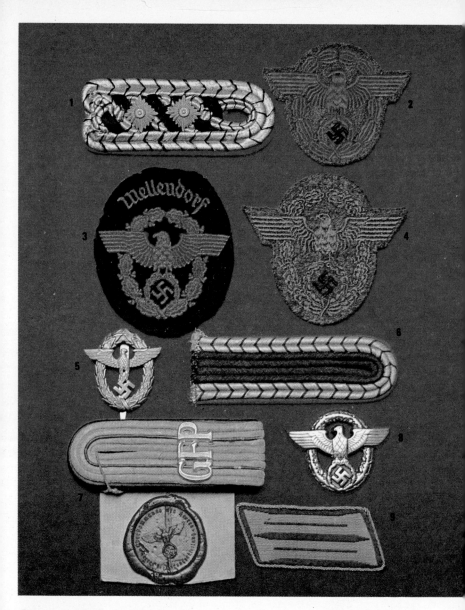

Selection of Police Items. **1** Shoulder strap of an inspector of the Schutzpolizei der Gemeinden (Municipal Police). **2** Sleeve badge of the Gendarmerie (Rural Police). **3** Sleeve badge of the Feurschutzpolizei (Fire Defence Police or Fire Brigade). **4** Sleeve badge of the Schutzpolizei des Reiches (City Police). **5** Police cap badge, first pattern. **6** Shoulder strap of a Wachmeister in the Gendarmerie. **7** Shoulder strap of a Leutnant in the Geheime Feld Polizei (Secret Military Police). (Tailor's sample for copying, with party seal of authentication). Attached to the Armed Forces in the field to detect spies, the GFP wore the uniform of the unit to which they were attached, plus the distinctive shoulder strap. **8** Police cap badge, second pattern. **9** Collar patch of a Haupwachtmeister in the Schutzpolizei des Reiches (City Police)

Walther PPK pistol carried by Nazi Party political leaders.

Sturmabteilung (SA) insignia. **1** Sleeveband of the 'Feldherrenhalle' regiment. **2** Dagger worn by all ranks from 1934. Inscription: 'All for Germany'. **3** Edelweiss badge worn on the cap by all members of the Alpine SA. **4** Swastika armband, worn on the sleeve by all ranks. **5** Belt buckle

Nazi armbands. 1 General Airforce Ordnance Artificer. 2 Real Estate Assessor. 3 Auxiliary police. 4 Armband worn by civilians and foreign workers employed by the Armed Forces. 5 Army traffic controller. 6 and 7 variations of civilians' and foreign workers' armband. 8 Army traffic regulation official

Nazi Election and Rally badges. *Top row, left:* Election badge, Lippe 1933.
Right: Election badge, Münster 1933. *Middle row, left:* Election badge 'Deutsch ist die Saar' (The Saar is German). *Right:* Rally badge commemorating Gau day of the NSDAP, June 1931. *Bottom row, left:* Rally badge commemorating the tenth anniversary of the Reichsparteitag (State Party Day) in Weimar. *Right:* Rally badge commemorating Kreistag (Kreis Day) in Mecklenburg

Rally badges. *Top left:* Labour Day emblem. *Top right :* Emblem for the National Party Rally, Nuremberg 1937 (Reichsparteitage). *Centre left :* NSPAD Kreistag 1938. *Centre right :* Emblem for Armed Forces Day 19th March 1939. *Bottom left :* Emblem for the Party Foundation Festival, Hamburg (Annual Oath Taking of political leaders), 24th February 1934. *Bottom right :* Emblem for the Labour Front Day, Bielefeld, 1933

Selection of Nazi Party badges. *Top row, left:* RAD Reichsarbeitsdienst (Labour Service) badge for men. *Right:* RAD badge for women. *Centre:* Badge of the NSFK – National Sozialistisches Fliegerkorps (Nazi Flying Corps). *Middle row, left:* Badge of the NSKK National socialistisches Kraftfahr Korps (Nazi Motor Cycle Corps). *Right:* Goldenes Parteiabzeichen (Gold Party badge), awarded to the first 100,000 Nazi Party members. *Bottom row, left:* Nazi Party badge worn by all members. *Centre:* Badge of the NS Frauenschaft (Nazi Mothers' Union). *Right:* Badge of the NS Altherrenbund der Deutschen Studenten (Organisation of former students of university and vocational schools and colleges) – top two badges inverted

Police shako badge

Political Leader's belt buckle. Worn on a brown leather belt in service dress and on a heavy gold brocade belt in full dress and some forms of walking out dress

Miscellaneous Nazi Awards. *Top left:* Grubenwohr Ehrenzeichen (mine rescue service medal). Awarded for life saving or for work in the mine rescue service. *Top right:* Luftschutz Ehrenzeichen (Civil Defence decoration) Second Class. Awarded for merit, and instituted in January 1938. There was also a First Class version which took the form of a cross. *Bottom left:* Ehrenzeichen des Deutschen Roten Kreuzes (German Red Cross decoration) 7th Grade. Instituted in seven classes in 1937 and awarded for meritorious service

Labour Awards. *Top:* Ehrenzeichen Pionier der Arbeit (Pioneer of Labour award). Instituted in 1940, this award was bestowed twice annually – on Labour Day and during the Party Rally at Nuremberg – for 'the highest efforts in the economic and social sphere'. Messerschmitt, Heinkel and Porsche were among recipients. *Bottom:* Dienstauszeichnung fur den Reicharbeitsdienst (Long Service Award of the RAD), instituted by Hitler and awarded in four classes: gilt medal with gilt eagle on the ribbon for twenty-five years service, silver medal with silver eagle on the ribbon for eighteen years, silver medal for twelve years and bronze medal for four years

Deutsches Olympiaehrenzeichen. (German Olympic Games Award, First Class.)
Instituted in 1936, it was worn at the throat on a 50mm ribbon. The Second Class
version was worn on the left breast on a 30mm ribbon. It was conferred on organisers
of the Eleventh Olympic Games in Berlin in 1936

Wehrmacht (Armed Forces) awards. *Left:* Ostfrontmedaille (Eastern Front medal), awarded to all German personnel who took part in the campaign on the Eastern Front between 15th November 1941 and 15th April 1942 and who had served at least fourteen days in combat or sixty days as non-combatants. *Right:* Deutsches Schutzwall Ehrenzeichen (German Westwall Defence medal), awarded to all personnel employed in the construction of the Atlantic wall

Verdienstkreuz I Stufe des Orden vom Deutchen Adler. (Order of the German Eagle, First Class.) Instituted on Labour Day 1937, this order was the only diplomatic order of Nazi Germany; it could be conferred on non-Germans

Selection of Nazi Party badges. *Top row, left :* Cap badge of an official of the DAF – Deutsche Arbeitsfront (German Labour Front. Membership was compulsory for all German workers.) *Right :* Commemoration badge of the SA Group's Aufmarsch (ceremonial parade) in Hamburg, April 1936. *Middle row, left :* Propaganda Ministry identification tag. *Right :* Cap badge of the NKOV – National Sozialistische Kriegsopferversorgung (War Disabled Welfare Organisation) founded in 1933 to care for war disabled, widows and orphans. *Bottom row, left :* Badge of the Military Administration, Belgium and Northern France. *Right :* Badge of a Doctors' Union Gau meeting at Münster on 19th August 1933

Ehrenzeichen der Deutschen Mutter (Cross of Honour of the German Mother). Awarded to the mothers of large families from December 1938. There were three classes – *Top:* Gilt award for eight or more children. *Bottom left:* Silver for six or seven children. *Bottom right:* Bronze for four children

Spanienkreuz (Spanish Cross). Awarded as a campaign decoration to Armed Forces personnel who took part in the Spanish Civil War, the majority of whom were from the Luftwaffe

Selection of long-service awards

Top: 12-year service cross of the SS
Bottom: 8-year service medal of the SS
Reverse showing the inscription

Top: 25-year service cross of the police
Bottom: 8-year service medal of the police

Dessert spoon from Hitler's personal dinner service

Hitler's personal letterhead

Gold stamp on cover of propaganda book

Crest over SS barracks gate

Politische Leiter Mütze (Political Leader's cap). There were four basic levels of political leadership: Reichleitung – the highest level, directly subordinate to Hitler, Gauleitung – a Gau was approximately equivalent in size to a county, Kreisleitung – each Gau was divided into a number of Kreise (in 1943 there were between five and forty-five Kreise in each Gau), Ortsgruppenleitung – each Kreis was again divided into several Ortsgruppen. Each level of leadership was denoted by coloured piping round the cap, collar and collar patches and round the edge of the armband. The white piping here denotes leadership at Kreis level

Gendarmerie Shako (Rural Police helmet). When worn with parade dress, a black horse hair plume was inserted behind the cockade drooping down to the left side of the helmet

SA other ranks' kepi

Luftwaffe General's summer cap

Artillery officer's cap (Army)

Luftwaffe OR's walking out dress cap with coloured identifying stripe: Brown—Signals, Yellow—Flying, Red—Artillery

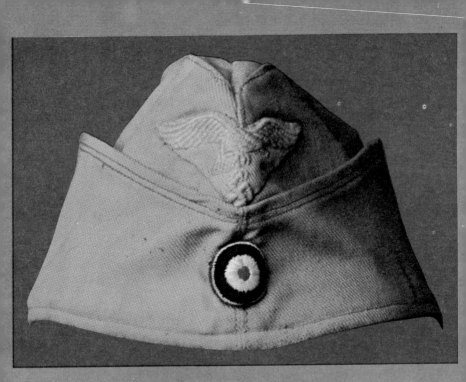

Luftwaffe OR's field cap worn in Africa

Army OR's field cap with coloured identifying stripe: Yellow—Cavalry, Pink—Panzer, Red—Artillery, White—Infantry

RAD (National Labour Service) Intermediate Leader's field cap

Luftwaffe OR's field cap

NSKK (National Motor Corps) OR's field cap

Luftwaffe OR's field cap 1944 pattern

Police field cap 1944 pattern

Civil defence helmet

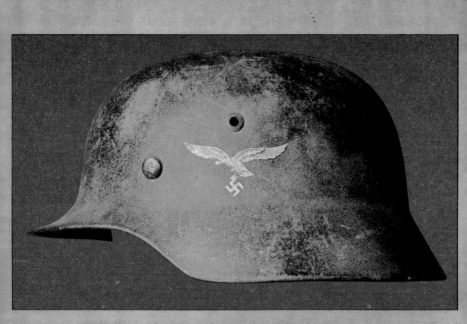

Luftwaffe steel helmet, 1935 pattern

Army steel helmet, 1916 pattern, modernised by the addition of Nazi emblem

Army steel helmet, 1935 pattern

Afrika Korps sun helmet

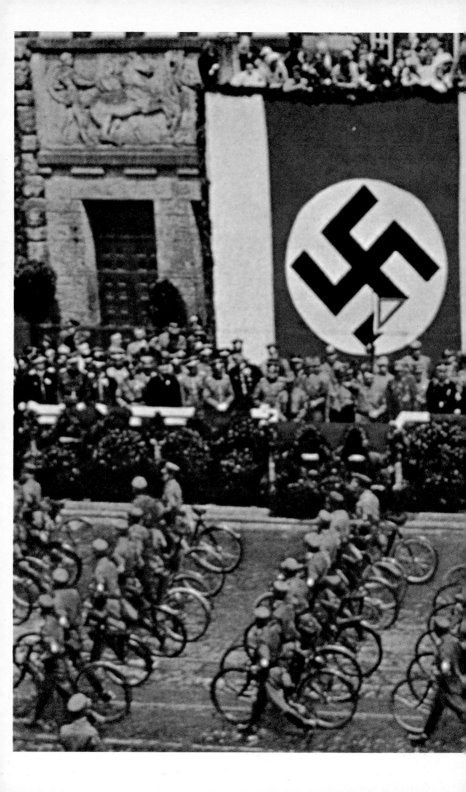

Duty uniform with blouse worn by all political leaders. Rank shown is that of senior assistant

Duty overcoat: always worn buttoned. Rank: assistant

Duty uniform, light brown
jacket, worn by all political
leaders. Rank: leader of an
NSDAP detachment

Duty uniform, white jacket, worn by
all political leaders. Rank: leader
of an NSDAP unit

Political leader's walking out uniform, single breasted light brown jacket. Rank: chief leader of a NSDAP detachment

Political leader's walking out uniform, double breasted light brown jacket. Rank: Senior duty organiser

Political leader's walking out uniform, single breasted white. Rank: district leader

Political leader's walking out uniform, single breasted white jacket. Rank: district leader

Duty overcoat, walking out
uniform. Rank: commander-in-
chief of the NSDAP

Cloak worn by commander-in-chief of the
NSDAP

litical leader's office
iform. Rank: chief work
ader

Office uniform with white jacket,
worn by chief and honorary political
leaders. Rank: leader of a task
force

**Bandmaster of a Main Territorial
(Gau) Band**

Bandsman of a Main Territorial Band

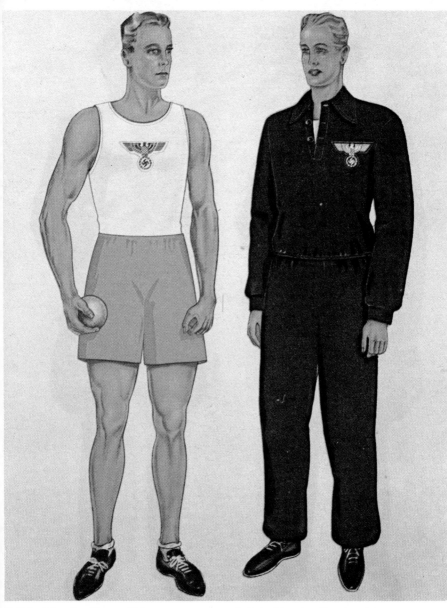

Political Leader (Sports kit)   **Political Leader (Track suit)**

**Group leader of 4-600 youths
at an Ordensburg NSDAP**

**Trainee leader of an Ordensburg
NSDAP**

Ordensburg were training schools responsible for the education of young party members
in world politics, general, mental and physical education for the NSDAP

German Labour Front political leader. Position: works foreman

German Labour Front: mess uniform

SA grand parade uniform; SA Senior Troop Leader

SA duty uniform; leader of an SA regiment

SA naval duty uniform; leader of SA
Naval Company 4 of the SA Naval
Regiment 9

SA duty uniform white; leader of SA
regiment, Staff Officer

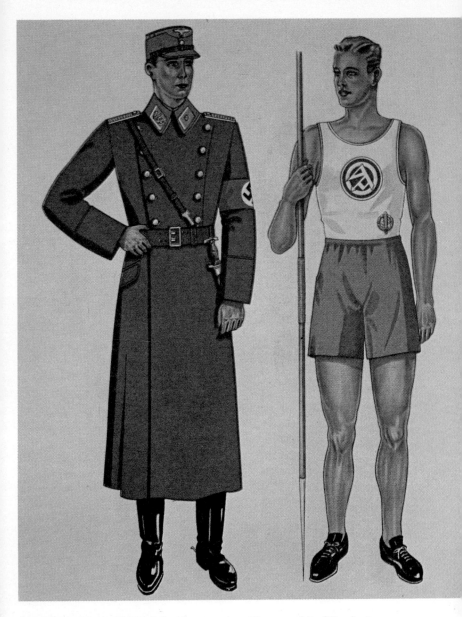

**SA duty overcoat; SA Troop Leader;
SA Cavalry Company**

SA sports kit; SA private

SA military uniform; SA Company Leader

SA military uniform; SA private

Political leader's duty overcoat, to be worn open. Rank: chief leader of a NSDAP unit

Political leader's overcoat for grand parades. Rank: senior leader of a NSDAP unit

National Motor Corps

Company Trooper; grand parade uniform
with crash helmet

Company Leader

**Duty uniform of the SS ; SS
Senior Troop Leader**

SS Under Troop Leader

Duty overcoat; SS corporal   Duty overcoat; SS colonel

Service dress of the army SS

Black service dress of the army SS; SS Troop Leader

Hitler Youth uniforms: *Left:* winter duty overcoat worn by the senior ranks. *Centre:* grand winter parade uniform. *Right:* grand summer parade uniform

Left: Dress uniform, female work leader. **Centre:** Working uniform; female worker. **Right:** Dress uniform; female worker

National Labour Service. *Left:* grand parade uniform of a work
leader. *Centre:* dress uniform of a senior work leader. *Right:*
working uniform of a voluntary workman

National Socialist Flying Corps

Corporal in grand parade uniform   Regiment leader in parade uniform

National Socialist Flying Corps

Regiment leader in walking out
uniform

Battalion leader in dress uniform

Top: Hitler's standard. *Bottom:* Flag of the 'Old Guard' of the NSDAP

National Flags of the NSDAP. *Top:* Administrative district within a territorial unit (Munich). *Bottom:* Local group within an administrative district (Altdorf)

Top : German labour front flag. ***Bottom*** : 'Model' industrial workshop flag, awarded for outstanding production

Top: SA standard 'Munich'. ***Bottom:*** SA company flag (1st company, Hitler's Bodyguard SA)

Top: National Motor Corps standard; the Motor Regiment M86. *Bottom:* National Motor Corps; company pennant of the Motor Company 4/M 82

Top: Standard of Hitler's Bodyguard Regiment SS 'Adolf Hitler'
Bottom: SS battalion flag 1st SS Regiment (Julius Schreck)

Top: SS Regiment 'Julius Schreck' (Munich)
Bottom: SS Cavalry Regiment (Munich)

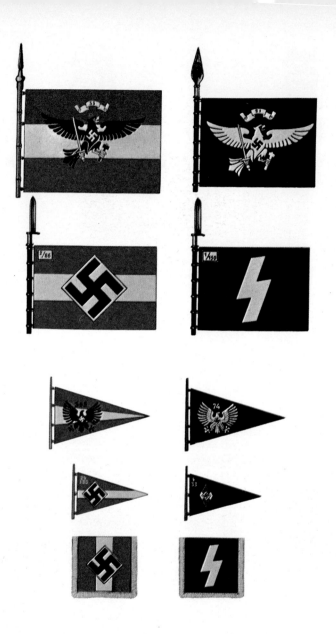

Flag of a sub-division of a Hitler Youth Region
Flag of a group of 160 HJ boys between ages 15/18 years
Hitler Youth (female); small territorial unit pennant
Hitler Youth (female); group pennant
Hitler Youth trumpet banner

Flag of a sub-division of a Hitler Youth Region (Young HJ)
Flag of a group of 160 HJ boys between the ages 10/14 (Young HJ)
Hitler Youth (female) Young HJ; small territorial unit pennant
Hitler Youth (female) Young HJ; group pennant
German Young People: trumpet banner

Top: A sub-division flag of the National Labour Service. *Bottom left:* Camp flag of the Men's National Labour Service. *Bottom right:* Camp flag of the Female Youth of the National Labour Service

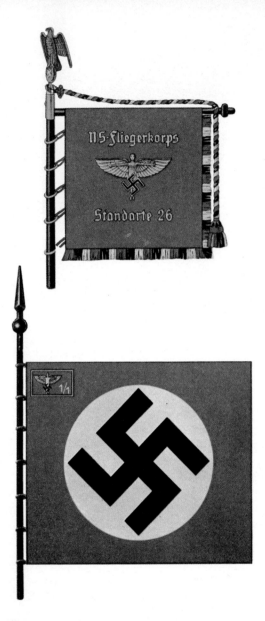

Top: Standard of Regiment 26 National Socialist Flying Corps. *Bottom:* Company flag (Company 1/1) National Socialist Flying Corps

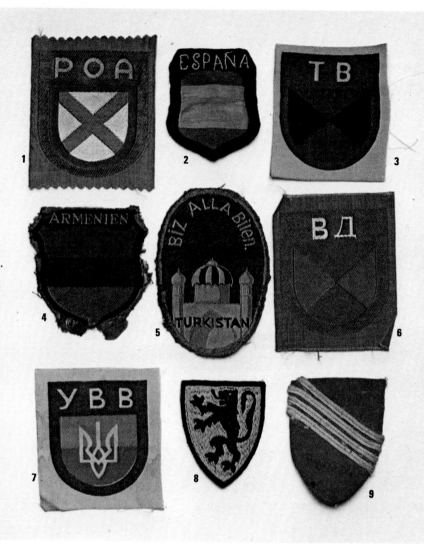

Selection of badges of the foreign volunteers in the German Armed Forces. 1 Badge of the Vlassov Army, composed of 'White' Russians, led by General Vlassov. This unit joined the Germans in 1942 to fight Bolshevism. 2 Badge of the 'Blue Division', composed of Spanish volunteers. 3 Badge of the Terek Cossacks. This unit was absorbed into the Waffen SS in 1944. 4 Badge of the Armenian Legion – disbanded in 1944. 5 Badge of the Turkistan Legion. Formed in 1942, this unit surrendered to the British in Italy in 1944. 6 Badge of the Don Cossacks – a component unit of the 1st Cossack Division. 7 Badge of the Ukranian Legion. This unit became part of the SS in 1944. 8 Badge of the 27th SS Volunteer Grenadier Division 'Langemark' – captured by the British in 1945. 9 Badge of the Latvian Legion – captured by the British in 1944

Naval insignia. 1 Insignia of non-commissioned ratings. 2 Cockade worn by midshipmen and warrant officers. 3 Sleeve badge of Naval Administration official. 4 Insignia of Naval Veterans Association. 5 Shoulder strap of boatswain in Naval Administration. 6 Naval War Destroyer's badge, awarded to crews for successful naval engagements. 7 Insignia for naval ratings. 8 Submarine war badge, reinstituted by Hitler and awarded to crews after two successful trips

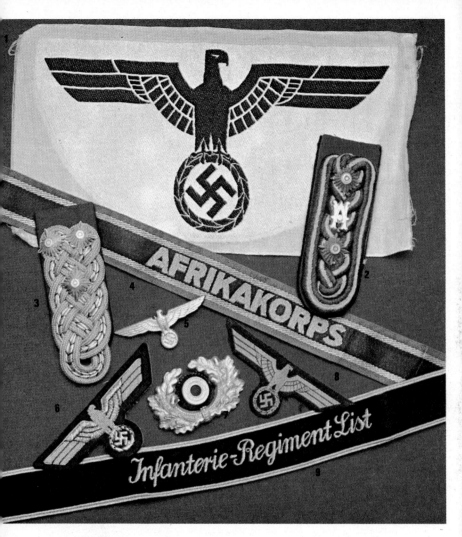

Army insignia. 1 Sports vest insignia. 2 Shoulder strap of an oberst in Army Administration. The dark red underlay shows that its wearer is an official of the Military Supreme Court. 3 Shoulder strap of a general in Army Administration, in this case a permanent official of the High Command. 4 Sleeveband worn by all personnel in the Afrika Korps. 5 Insignia worn on the walking out dress cap by all other ranks and NCOs. 6 Insignia worn on the right breast by all officers up to the rank of major-general 7 Cockade also worn on the walking out dress cap by other ranks and NCOs. 8 Insignia worn above the right breast pocket of field dress by other ranks and NCOs. 9 Sleeveband of the Grenadier Regiment No 199. Hitler had served in this regiment during the First World War

Luftwaffe insignia. 1 Marksman's lanyard, 7th grade, worn from the right shoulder to the second tunic button in all branches except the anti-aircraft artillery, who wore miniature artillery shells instead of acorns to denote grade. 2 Insignia worn on the right breast of all tunics by NCOs and other ranks. 4 Emblem of the German Air Sports Association, forerunner of the Luftwaffe. Worn on the upper left arm. 5 Collar patch of an Oberleutnant in the anti-aircraft artillery reserve. 6 Sleeve badge of an Unteroffizier worn on both sleeves of overalls and flying suits. 7 Emblem worn above the cockade on walking out dress cap by NCOs and other ranks. 8 Collar patch of a Leutnant in the signals branch. 9 Luftwaffe anti-aircraft badge

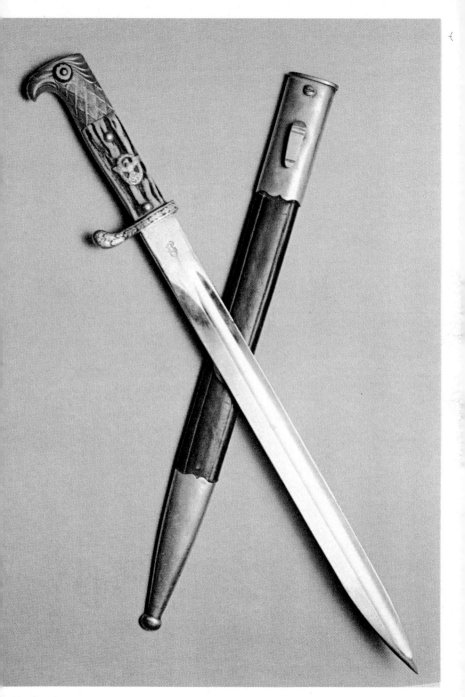

Nazi Police dress bayonet

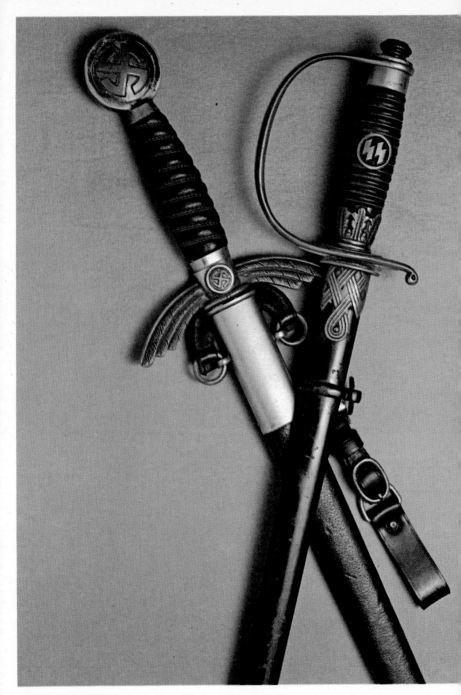

Left: Luftwaffe sword, worn by officers and NCOs. *Right:* SS sword, presented to SS officers by Himmler for meritorious service

1 Other ranks belt buckle of the HJ. 2 Other ranks belt buckle of the Army. 3 Other ranks belt buckle of the Luftwaffe. 4 Other ranks belt buckle of the early SS units in the Essen Area

1 SS other ranks belt buckle. 2 German Air Sport Association other ranks belt buckle. 3 RAD other ranks belt buckle (inverted). 4 SA other ranks belt buckle

Roll of Honour clasps. These were awarded to Armed Forces personnel who already held the Iron Cross. First and Second Class for individual acts of bravery. *Top left:* Navy. *Top right:* Airforce. *Bottom:* Army. The ribbons were worn in the second buttonhole of the tunic

Army marksman's award. *Left:* Lanyard with badge for artillery, infantry and cavalry. (*Right:* Badge for Panzer units.) Awarded in twelve grades, indicated by the addition of swords to the shield, the colour of the badge and the addition of small acorns to the cord. Worn from the right shoulder strap to the second button on the tunic in all uniforms except field dress

Naval Awards. *Top left:* Naval destroyer's war badge. Awarded for a number of successful naval engagements and instituted after June 1940. *Top right:* War badge for minesweepers, submarinechasers and escort vessels. Awarded for three operational sorties. *Bottom left:* Auxiliary cruiser's war badge. The 'auxiliary cruisers' were armed vessels disguised as neutral cargo ships which operated as surface raiders. This badge was awarded on the completion of a long, successful voyage. *Bottom right:* High Seas Fleet war badge, awarded for a successful naval engagement or for twelve weeks' active service at sea

Army Awards. *Left:* General assault badge. Instituted in June 1940 and awarded for assaults made on three different days. *Right:* Anti-aircraft badge. Instituted in July 1941, this had similar service requirements to its Luftwaffe counterpart. *Bottom:* Anti-partisans war badge. Instituted by Himmler on 30th January 1944 and awarded in three grades – gilt for 150 days, silver for fifty days and bronze for twenty days active service

Wound badge. Reinstituted by Hitler in 1939 and awarded in three classes. *Left:* Gilt for five or more wounds, for total disablement or permanent blindness. *Right:* Silver for three or four wounds or for the loss of a hand, foot or eye or for deafness. *Bottom:* Black for one or two wounds

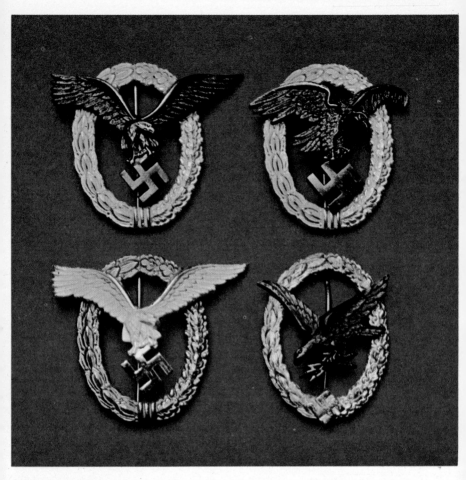

Air Awards. *Top left:* Pilot's badge, instituted by Göring on 26th March 1936, and awarded on completion of training. *Top right:* Observer's badge. Also instituted on 26th March 1936, this was awarded after two month's non-operational flying service, or for five sorties. *Bottom left:* Combined pilot and observer badge. Also instituted on 26th March 1936, this was awarded to personnel who had held the above two badges for at least a year. *Bottom right:* Wireless operator and air gunner's badge. This badge was instituted on the same date as the previous three, and had the same service requirements as the observer's badge

Air Awards. *Top left:* Army Parachutist's badge. Instituted in 1937, it was awarded on completion of training. *Top right:* Airforce Parachutist's badge. Instituted in November 1936 and awarded on completion of training. Waffen SS parachute troops wore this badge. *Centre:* Commemorative badge for ex-airmen, instituted in 1936 for all ex-fighting personnel who had been honourably discharged from aircrew duties. *Bottom left:* Airforce anti-aircraft war badge. Awarded on a points basis for the destruction of Allied aircraft or for individual acts of merit. *Bottom right:* Ground assault badge of the airforce. Awarded to all ground combat formations of the Luftwaffe who were eligible for an army assault badge

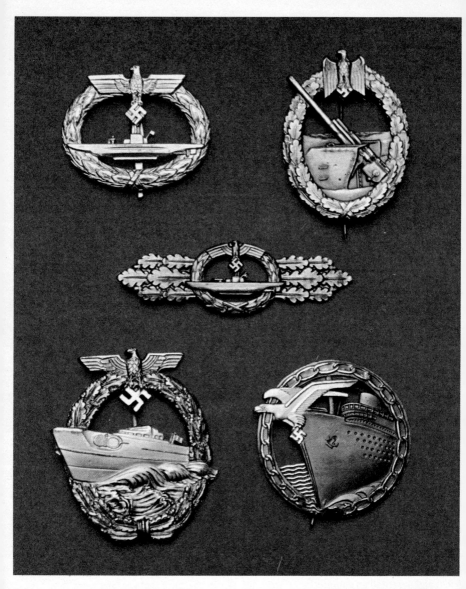

Naval Awards. *Top left:* Submarine war badge. Reinstituted by Hitler to be awarded to U-Boat crews who had made two successful operational trips. *Top right:* Naval Coast Artillery war badge. Awarded on a points basis for the successful destruction of enemy aircraft. *Centre:* Submarine combat clasp – a higher grade submarine war badge. *Bottom left:* E-Boat war badge. Awarded to E-Boat crews who had participated in at least twelve sorties. *Bottom right:* Blockade runners' badge. Awarded to the crews of merchant vessels who successfully avoided the Allied blockade

Army Awards. *Top left:* Infantry assault badge. Awarded only to Infantry and Mountain Infantry, it demanded the same service requirements as the general assault badge. *Top right:* Infantry assault badge – a special version awarded to motorised infantry. *Bottom left:* Tank assault badge. Awarded for three tank engagements on different days. *Bottom right:* Tank assault badge – later version after grades were instituted for 100, seventy-five, fifty and twenty-five (shown here) engagements

Service dress tunic of a Leutnant in the Luftwaffe. On the left breast pocket is the Iron Cross First Class of the First World War and the Wound Badge. On the buttonhole is the ribbon of the War Merit Cross Second Class

Parade tunic of a Hauptmann in the Infantry. The white underlay on the collar denotes the Arm of Service. This is repeated on the cuff patches, shoulder straps and as piping round the collar and down the front of the tunic. The parade uniform was seldom worn after the outbreak of war

Service dress tunic of a Volkssturm (Home Defence Unit) Batallionführer. A variety of uniforms was worn; the tunic shown is that of a Reichswehr (German Army of the Weimar Republic). The collar shows distinctive Volkssturm patches, bearing the rank insignia. The sleeveband incorporates the National Insignia; the buttonhole ribbon is that of the Iron Cross, 2nd Class (First World War): bar denotes subsequent award of a Second Class Nazi Iron Cross

War Merit Cross. Instituted in October 1939 and awarded for deeds which did not merit an Iron Cross. When awarded with swords it was given for military merit other than in battle and for bravery other than in the front line. Without swords it was given for significant contributions to the war effort. *Top:* Knights Cross with Swords. *Left:* First Class without Swords. *Right:* Second Class without Swords. *Bottom:* War Merit Medal. This was conferred only on civilians

Top : Knights Cross with Oakleaves and Swords. *Bottom left :* Iron Cross, First Class (Bar above). *Bottom right :* Iron Cross, Second Class

Long Service Awards. *Top row:* Faithful Service Award. *Left to right:* Fifty years service, forty years service, twenty-five years service. Instituted in 1938, it was awarded for work in the public services. *Bottom row:* Armed Forces Long Service Award. *Left:* Twenty-five years service. *Right:* Eighteen years service. Instituted in 1936 and awarded to members of all three services

Close Combat Award of the Army. *Top:* Gilt for fifty days. *Centre:* Silver for thirty days. *Bottom:* Bronze for fifteen days. This award was instituted in 1942 for participation in hand-to-hand fighting without the support of armour

SS field cap, 1943 pattern

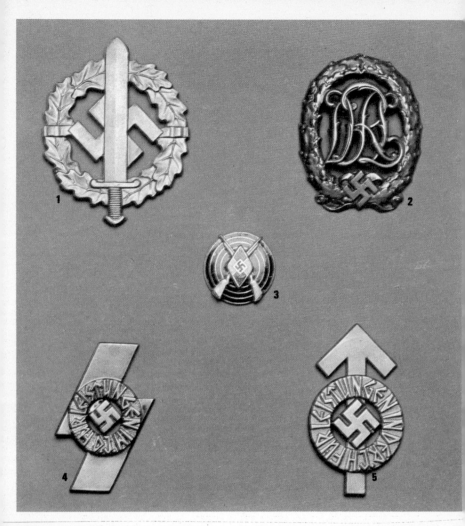

1 SA sports badge in silver. Awarded for proficiency tests generally of a military nature.
2 Sports badge in bronze. Awarded for proficiency tests not specifically of a military
nature. SS candidates had to qualify for the above two badges before they were finally
accepted into the SS. 3 Hitler Youth Shooting Award for proficiency in shooting small
bore weapons. 4 Hitler Youth Proficiency Award for those 10 to 14 years old.
5 Hitler Youth Proficiency Award for members 15 to 18 years old

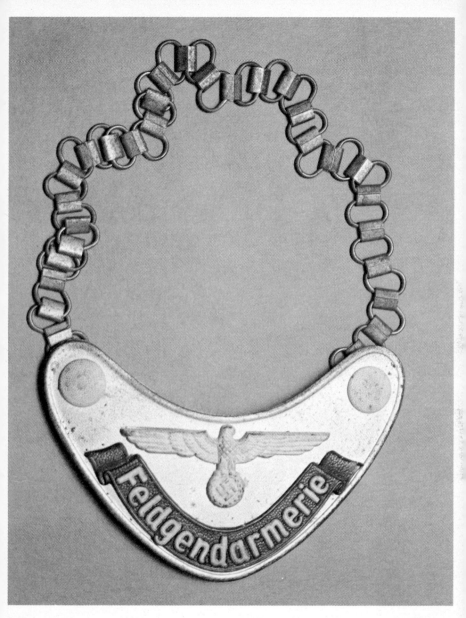

Military Police gorget. This was worn on night duty by military police and was treated with luminous paint on the buttons, eagle, and lettering so that it was easily visible in the dark

Volksturm 1945

Es ist nicht schwer in guten Tagen
Das Fahnentuch voran zu tragen
Der stolzen Reihe,
Erst wenn im Sturm die Fetzen knattern
Der müde Haufe will zerflattern
Zeigt sich die Treue.

Josef Hieß

'It is not hard on a good day
To carry the flag high
In proud ranks;
When in the storm the flag flies in shreds
The weary will lose heart
Then the true spirit shows'

This poster, written in poor patriotic German, was found in Berlin just after the collapse

Lfde. Nr.	Name, Vorname	Degen	Ring	J.Zr.	Reichs.Z.	Ehrenzeichen	Dienststellung	Partei-Nr. 1—1,8 Mill.	über 1,8 Mill.	₷₷-Nr.	Geburts-datum
1	Himmler Heinrich, R.L., St.Rat, M.d.R.	⚔	O	⬤	⬤	Y	Reichsführer-₷₷ u Chef der deutschen Polizei	14 303	—	168	7. 10. 00

₷₷-Obergruppenführer:

2	Schwarz Franz Xaver, R.L., M.d.R.	⚔	O	—	—		Stab RF ₷₷	6	—	38 500	27. 11. 75
3	Dietrich Josef, ⬤I St.Rat., M.d.R.	⚔	O	⬤	⬤	Y	F. Da. Ost u. Leib-standarte-₷₷	89 015	—	1 177	28. 5. 92
4	Weitzel Fritz, St.Rat., Po.Pr., M.d.R.	⚔	O	⬤	⬤	Y	F. Da. West	18 833	—	408	27. 4. 04
5	Daluege Kurt, ✠II St.Rat., M.d.R.	⚔	O			Y	Stab RF ₷₷, m. d. Range eines Haupt-amtschefs	31 981	—	1 119	15. 9. 97
6	Darré Walther, ✠II R.Mi., R.L., M.d.R.	⚔	O	a	a	Y	Chef Ru.S.-Hauptamt	248 256	—	6 882	14. 7. 95
7	Buch Walter, ✠I R.L., M.d.R.	⚔	O	—	—	Y	Stab RF ₷₷	7 733	—	81 353	24. 10. 83
8	von Woyrsch Udo, ✠I St.Rat., M.d.R.	⚔	O	⬤	⬤	Y	Stab RF ₷₷	162 349	—	3 689	24. 7. 95
9	Krüger Friedrich-Wilhelm, ✠I St.Rat., M.d.R.	⚔	O	⬤		Y	Insp. Grenz- u. Wacheinheiten	171 199	—	6 123	8. 5. 94
10	Erbprinz zu Waldeck und Pyrmont Josias, ✠I M.d.R.	⚔	O	k	k	Y	F. Da. Fulda-Werra	160 025	—	2 139	13. 5. 96
11	Amann Max, ✠II R.L., M.d.R.	⚔	O				Stab RF ₷₷	3	—	53 143	24. 11. 91
12	Frhr. von Eberstein Karl, ✠I Po.Pr., M.d.R.	⚔	O	a	a	Y	F. Da. Süd	15 067	—	1 386	14. 1. 94
13	Bouhler Philipp, ✠II R.L., M.d.R.	⚔	O	k	k		Stab RF ₷₷	12	—	54 932	11. 9. 99
14	Jeckeln Friedrich, ✠II M.d.R.	⚔	O	⬤		Y	F. Da. Mitte	163 348	—	4 367	2. 2. 95
15	Lorenz Werner, ✠I St.Rat., M.d.R.	⚔	O	⬤		Y	Stab RF ₷₷	317 994	—	6 636	2. 10. 91
16	Heißmeyer August, ✠I M.d.R.	⚔	O	⬤		Y	Chef ₷₷-Hauptamt	21 573	—	4 370	11. 1. 97
17	Schmauser Heinrich, ✠I M.d.R.	⚔	O	k	k	Y	F. Da. Main	245 704	—	3 359	18. 1. 90

₷₷-Gruppenführer:

18	Weinreich Hans, ✠I M.d.R.	⚔	O				Stab RF ₷₷	5 920	—	278 160	5. 9. 96
19	Wittje Kurt, ✠I M.d.R.	⚔	O			Y	Stab RF ₷₷	256 189	—	5 870	2. 10. 94
20	Dr. Dietrich Otto, ✠I R.L., St.Sek., M.d.R.	⚔	O				Stab RF ₷₷	126 727	—	101 349	31. 8. 97
21	Forster Albert, G.L., M.d.R.	⚔	O				Stab RF ₷₷	1 924	—	158	26. 7. 02

First page of the SS staff list. Every SS Officer was listed in this book

Beförderungsdatum: 9. November 1939

Ernennung
zum „SS-Mann" frühestens: ----

Berlin, den 13. Dezember 1939

Der Reichsführer-SS

H. Himmler.

Der Führer des SS-Oberabschnitts
Alpenland

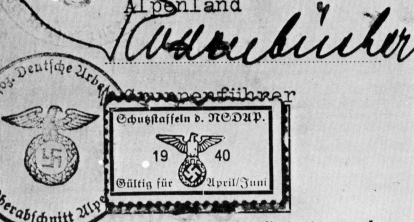

SS ID card

Schutzstaffel der N.S.D.A.P.

SS=Unterführer= Ausweis Nr. 301 812

Partei=Mitglieds=Nr.

Pregler Rudolf

geboren am 24.12.1895

ist SS-Oberscharführer

im 9/38. SS-Standarte.

Eigenhändige Unterschrift

SSV K 15

SS ID card

Equivalent Ranks in Party and Military Organisations

BRITISH/U.S. ARMY	GERMAN POLICE	NSDAP	SS	GERMAN ARMY
Field-Marshal US General of Army	No equivalent	Reichsleiter Hauptbefehlsleiter	Reichsführer	Generalfeldmarschall
No equivalent	Generaloberst der Polizei	Reichsleiter Hauptbefehlsleiter	Oberstgruppenführer (from 1942 only)	Generaloberst
General	General der Polizei	Gauleiter Oberbefehlsleiter	Obergruppenführer	General
Lieutenant-General	Generalleutnant der Polizei	Gauleiter (or deputy) Befehlsleiter	Gruppenführer	Generalleutnant

Major-General	Generalmajor der Polizei	Gauleiter (or deputy) Hauptdienstleiter	Brigadeführer	Generalmajor
Brigadier US Brigadier-General	Oberst der Schutzpolizei or Gendarmerie	Gauleiter (or deputy) Oberdienstleiter	Oberführer	Oberst
Colonel	Reichskriminaldirektor	Gauleiter (or deputy) Oberdienstleiter	Standartenführer	Oberst
Lieutenant-Colonel	Oberstleutnant der Schupo or Gendarmerie Oberregierungs und Kriminalrat	Kreisleiter Dienstleiter or Hauptbereichsleiter	Oberstürmbannführer	Oberstleutnant
Major	Major der Schutzpolizei or Gendarmerie Regierungs-und Kriminalrat Kriminaldirecktor	Kreisleiter Oberbereichsleiter Bereichsleiter Hauptabschnittsleiter Ortsgruppenleiter Oberabschnittsleiter	Stürmbannführer	Major
Captain	Hauptmann der Schutzpolizei or Gendarmerie Kriminalrat	Ortsgruppenleiter Abschnittsleiter Zellenleiter Hauptgemeinschaftsleiter Obergemeinschaftsleiter	Haupstürmführer	Hauptmann Rittmeister
Lieutenant US 1st Lieutenant	Oberleutnant der Schutzpolizei or Gendarmerie Kriminalkommissar Kriminalinspektor	Zellenleiter Gemeinschaftsleiter Blockleiter Haupteinsatzleiter	Oberstürmführer	Oberleutnant

Second Lieutenant	Leutnant der Schutzpolizei or Gend. Kriminalsekretar Kriminaloberassistent	Bleckleiter Obereinsatzleiter Einsatzleiter	Unterstürmführer	Leutnant
Regimental Sergeant-Major US Sergeant-Major	Meister Kriminalsekretar	Hauptbereitschaftsleiter	Stürmscharführer	Stabsfeldwebel Stabswachtmeister
Sergeant-Major	Hauptwachmeister Kriminaloberassistent	Hauptbereitschaftsleiter	Stabsscharführer (Waffen-SS)	Hauptfeldwebel Hauptwachtmeister
Sergeant-Major US Master-Sergeant	Kompaniehauptwachtmeister Kriminaloberassistent	Oberbereitschaftsleiter	Hauptscharführer	Oberfeldwebel Oberwachtmeister
Quartermaster-Sergeant US Technical Sergeant	Revieroberwachtmeister Kriminalassistent	Bereitschaftsleiter	Oberscharführer	Feldwebel Wachtmeister
Staff Sergeant	Oberwachtmeister Kriminalassistent	Bereitschaftsleiter	Scharführer	Unterfeldwebel
Sergeant	Wachtmeister Kriminalassistentanwarter	Hauptarbeitsleiter	Unterscharführer	Unteroffizier
Corporal	Rottwachtmeister	Oberarbeitsleiter	Rottenführer	Stabsgefreiter Obergefreiter Gefreiter
Lance-Corporal US Private 1st Class	Unterwachtmeister	Arbeitsleiter Oberhelfer	Stürmmann	Oberschütze
Private	Anwarter	Helfer	SS-Mann	Schütze

Glossary

Abschnitt
Regional subdivision of the territorial organisation of the SS, Also regional HQ of the SD

Abt Landesverteidigung
The National Defence Branch in the OKW

Abtielung
A branch, section or subdivision of a main department or office. Also a military unit or detachment up to battalion strength

Abwehr
Espionage, Counter espionage and Sabotage Service of the German High Command

Abwehrpolizei
Counter espionage police, part of the Grenzpolizei controlled by the Gestapo

Abzeichen
Appointment, Badge of Rank or distinction

Ahnenerbe Forschungs und Lehrgeminsschaft
Society for research into and Teaching of Ancestral Heritage. It promoted the study and teaching of Nazi racial theories; administered by the SS

Allgemeine SS
The main body of the SS composed of full and part time, inactive and honorary members. Distinct from the Waffen SS

Amt
Main office or directorate of a ministry

Amt VI
Foreign intelligence service of the SD

Amtsgericht
Law court

Amtsgruppe
Branch of an Hauptamt

Anhaltelager
Temporary detention camp

Anordnung
A regulation or an order

Anwarter
SS cadet or candidate

Arbeitseinsatzführer
Chief supervisor of labour in a concentration camp

Armee Oberkommando
An Army HQ

Aufklürung
Military Reconnaissance

Ausbildung
Training

Auslands Organization
NSDAP agency for the supervision of Germans living abroad. Ranked as a Gaue

Aussendienststelle
Outpost of the Sipo and SD

Aussenkommando
A working detachment of prisoners living outside a concentration camp

ausser Dienst
Retired

Auswrütiges Amt
The Ministry of Foreign Affairs

Bahnschutzpolizei
Railway protection police with auxiliary status. Became part of the SS in 1942

Bann
A subdivision of a Hitler Youth region

Barbarossa
Code name for the German attack on Russia on the 22nd June 1941

Bauinspektion
Building inspectorate controlled by the WVHA

Bauwesen
Branch of the WVHA which controlled forced labour by concentration camp prisoners on works and buildings

Beamter
Functionary

Beauftragter
Commissioner or administrator

Befehl
Command or order

Befehlshaber der Ordnungspolizei
Commander of the uniformed police at regional level in occupied territories

Befehlshaber der Sicherheitspolizei und des Sicherheitsdientes
Commander of the Security Police and Security Service in occupied territories

Bekanntmachung
A proclamation

Bereitschaft
An emergency police or NSDAP detachment

Bewachungsmannschaft
An SS guard detachment in a concentration camp

Berlin Police Bureau 1A
Forerunner of the Gestapo

Blockführer
(a) Lowest NSDAP official responsible for the political supervision of 50 households
(b) An SS NCO in charge of a block of concentration camp prisoners

Capo or Kapo
A works foreman of a concentration camp labour force usually a common as opposed to a political criminal

Chef des Generalstabes des Heeres
Chief of the Army General Staff

Chef der Sicherheitspolizei und des SD
Chief of the Security Police and Security Service. Heydrich to 1942 then Kaltenbrunner

Chef der Zivilverwaltung
Chief of civil administration in an occupied territory

Chefsache
Top secret document

Deutsche Arbeitsfront
The German Labour Front NSDAP organisation of professional associations and guilds Chief: Robert Ley

Deutsche Ausrustungswerke
Equipment factory established by the SS in 1939

Deutsche Sportabzeichen
Nazi sports certificate

Deutsche Erd und Steinwerke GmbH
Brickworks company set up by the SS in 1938 using forced labour

Deutsche Rotes Kreuz
German Red Cross controlled indirectly by the SS

Dienstvorschrift
Regulation or a service manual

Durchgangslager
Transit camp

Ehrenführer
Honorary SS general

Einheit
A unit

Einsatzgruppe
An operational task force of the SD and Sipo for special missions into occupied territory

Endlösung, die
The Final Solution. The name used for the mass killing of the Jews

Ersatzheer
The replacement army

Feldlagerkorps
Shock group of the SA disbanded in 1935 and incorporated into the police

Feuerschutzpolizei
Fire fighting police

Feuerwehren
Fire brigade

Flüchtlingslager
Refugee camp

Fordernde Mitglieder der SS
Patron member of the SS paying regular contributions to SS funds

Freiwilliger
A volunteer

Führer
A leader

Führerhauptquartier
Hitler's field HQ

Führungshauptamt
The operations department of the SS in charge of the organisation and employment of its formations

Gaue
The main territorial unit of the NSDAP Germany was divided into 42 Gaue. The Auslands-Organisation was the 43rd

Gauleiter
NSDAP official in charge of a Gaue Responsible for civil all economic and political affairs, civil defence and the organisation of labour

Geheime Staatspolizei
See Gestapo

Geheimes Staatspolizeiamt
See Gestapa

Gemeindepolizei
Municipal Police

Gendarmerie
Rural Police, including motorised unit for traffic control

Generalquartiermeister des Heeres
The Quartermaster General of the Army

Germanische SS
The Germanic formations of the Waffen SS

Gestapo
The Secret State Police Amt Ia of the RSHA

Gestapa
The National HQ of the Gestapo became part of RSHA in 1939

Gewerbepolizei
Control of trade establishments and the application of price controls

Grenzpolizei or Grepo
Frontier control police, controlled by the SD, they wore SS uniform

Grenzüberwachung
SSG units which reinforced the Grenzpolizei, disbanded in 1937 and absorbed into the Grepo

Häftling
A prisoner

Hakenkreuz
The swastika, emblem of the nazi party. From 1935 the emblem of the Third Reich

Hauptamt SS
Central office of the SS responsible for welfare, education, recruitment and training of the SS

Hauptamt SS Gericht
Legal department responsible for SS law and discipline within the SS

Haupttreuhandstelle Ost
A public corporation which organised the seizure of Jewish and Polish property, created by Göring

Heer
Army

Hilfsgrenzangestellte
Pre 1939 auxiliary frontier personal used to reinforce the customs service

Hilfspolizei or Hipo
SS and SA men deputized into the regular police force

Hitler Jugend or HJ
The Hitler Youth formed in 1935 from the junior branch of the SA

Hoherer SS und Polizeiführer
Senior SS and Police commander of a Werhkreis

Hoheitsabzeichen
National Badge, the Nazi eagle worn on the left arm of the police and the SS, and on the right breast of the Wehrmacht

Hoheitsträgder
A Nazi party official

Ic-Dienst
Intelligence Service of the SS, started by Heydrich, the forerunner of the SD

Jagdverbände
SS sabotage units employed in occupied territories. Its chief was Otto Skorzeny

Junkerschule
An officer cadet training school for the SS

Kasernierte Polizei
Militarised barrack police

Kommandofuhrer
NCO in charge of a party of prisoners working outside a concentration camp

Konzentrationslager
Concentration camp

Kreis
Administrative district within a Gaue

Kriesleiter
The lowest paid official of the Nazi party. Responsible for a Kries

Kriegsgefangener
A prisoner of war

Kriminalpolizei or Kripo
The criminal police, which with the Gestapo, formed the Security Police (Sipo). Became the Amt V of the RSHA in 1939

Lager
A camp

Lagerkommandant
The chief officer of a concentration camp

Landwacht
Auxiliary rural police established in 1942 to help the regular police.
Mostly ex servicemen from the Great War.

Lebensborn
Fount of Life maternity homes for both married and unmarried mothers
of SS fathered children. Promoted Nazi racial ideas. Paid for by
deductions from SS men's pay, single men paying most.

Leibstandarte SS Adolf Hitler
Hitler's bodyguard regiment, it was the first militarized SS formation.
Formed in 1933 from the Stabswache Berlin, it reached divisional
strength in 1941. Fought on the Western and Russian fronts

Leibwache
Bodyguard

Leiter
The leader or chief of an office or authority

Luftschutzpolizei
The air raid protection police established in 1942.

Machtergreifung, die
Nazi word for the 'seizure of power' on the 30th January 1933

Marktpolizei
Market police. Responsible for the control of markets and fairs

Meldewesen
Police registration

Max Heiliger
Name of an account in the Reichbank for money made from
confiscated valuables and gold teeth of concentration camp inmates

Militarbefehlshaber
Military governor of an occupied territory

Mitglied
Member

Night and Fog
The title of the order given by the OKW in December 1941. Persons in occupied countries found guilty of any activity against the Third Reich or its representatives, would be deported to Germany. They would be tried by special courts and kept in concentration camps.

Nationalsozialistische Deutsche Arbeiter Partei or NSDAP
The Nazi Party's full title. The National Socialist German Worker's Party

Nationalpolitische Erziehungsanstalten or Napola
National Political Educational Institutes, controlled by the SS and run on Hitler Youth lines. Secondary school level.

Nationalsozialistische Kraftfahr-Korps or NSKK
The National Motor Corps, a para-military formation of the Nazi Party

Nationalsozialistische Volkswohlfahrt or NSV
The National Socialist Peoples Welfare Organization

Oberbefehlshaber des Heeres
The Commander-in-chief of the Army. Brauchitsch 1938 to 41, Hitler 1941 to 45

Oberkommando des Heeres or OKH
The High Command of the Army

Oberkommando der Wehrmacht OKW
The High Command of the Armed Forces. Hitler was the supreme commander and Keitel was the chief

Oberste SA Führer
The supreme commander of the SA. Hitler from 1930, Pfeffer Von Salomon before that

Oberste SA Führung
The High Command of the SA

Ordnungspolizei
The Order Police, the regular uniformed police. Comprising the Schutzpolizei, the Gendarmerie, the Feuerschutzpolizei and various technical and auxiliary services

Organisation Todt
A semi-military organisation established in 1933, for the construction of Autobahn and military installations.

Ortspolizei
The local police

Persönlicher Stab RfSS
Himmler's Personal Staff, ranking as a Hauptamt of the SS

Politische Leiter
Political leader. A senior official of the Nazi Party

Polizeidivision
A fully militarised formation of the Waffen-SS, established in 1939
from the regular police

Rapportführer
An NCO in the SS responsible for taking roll-calls in a concentration
camp

Rasse-und Siedlungshauptamt
The Central Office for Race and Settlement, run by the SS. It was
supposed to control the racial purity of the SS and organise the
settlement of SS colonists in the conquered eastern territories

Reichsarbeitsdienst
The National Labour Service

Reichführer-SS and Chef der Deutschen Polizei
Reich Chief of the SS and Head of the German Police. A title created for
Himmler in 1936

Reichsführung-SS
The Supreme Command of the SS

Reichskanzler
The Chancellor of the Reich. Adolf Hitler

Reichssicherheitsdienst
A special Security Service for guarding Hitler and the leading members
of the Nazi Party. Recruited from the criminal police

Reichssicherheitshauptamt or RSHA
The Central Security Department of the Reich, consisting of the
Gestapo, Kripo, and the SD. Established in 1939

Reichskriegsflagge
A voluntary para-military organisation led by Roehm, which joined
forces with Hitler during the Munich Putch. It formed the nucleus of
the SA or Brownshirts

Reichswehr
The 100,000 man army which Germany was limited to by the Treaty of
Versailles. The limit was exceded secretly, and this part of the army
was known as the Schwarze Reichswehr, or Black Reichswehr. In May
1935 the name was changed to the Wehrmacht when the treaty was
renounced

Sanitätsdienst
Medical Service

Salon Kitty
High class brothel established by Heydrich in Berlin for foreign diplomats and senior Nazi Partymembers. It had nine bedrooms with hidden microphones which were used for gathering incriminating or embarrassing evidence for blackmail or other purposes by Heydrich

Schutzhaft
Protective custody

Schutzhaftlager
Concentration camp

Schutzmannschaft
Auxillary police in the Eastern Occupied Territories recruited from the local population

Schutzpolizei
The regular uniforms municipal and country police which formed the bulk of the Ordnungspolizei

Schutzstaffel
The SS. Literally Protection Detachment, formed in 1925 from the Stosstrupp Hitler

Selbstschutz
a) A self help militia recruited by the SS from the Volksdeutsche in Poland
b) A German nationalist self protection organization. Pre 1925
c) The self protection service, part of the Luftschutzdienst made up of air raid wardens

Sicherheitsdienst des RfSS or SD
The Security Branch of the SS formed in 1932 under Heydrich. The intelligence Organization of the NSDAP

Sicherheitshauptamt or SD Hauptamt
The SS Central Security Department

Sicherheispolizei
Security Police. Made up of the Gestapo and the Kripo under Heydrich

Sigrunen
The runic double S insignia of the SS

Sonderbehandlung
Special treatment. Nazi bureaucratic term for killing prisoners

Sonderkommando
Special detachment of the SS for police and political tasks

Staatsschutzkorps
A semi-official term for the combined functions of the Gestapo, Kripo and SD for the protection of the state

Stab
A staff

Stabswache
The original Party HQ guard, formed from the SA in 1923 and later merged into the Stosstrupp Adolf Hitler

Stahlhelm
Steel helmets. Nationalist ex-serviceman's organization formed at the end of the '14-'18 war by Franz Seldte. Compulsorily absorbed into the SA in 1933

Schwarze Reichswehr
See Reichswehr

Stammlager or Stalag
A permanent prisoner of war camp

Standarte
An SS or SA formation roughly the size of a regiment

Standrecht
Martial law

Stosstrupp
Shock troop

Streifendienst
The Hitler Youth Patrol Service officered by the SS

Sturm
An SS or SA formation roughly the size of a company

Sturmabteilungen
The SA, or Brownshirts or Stormtroopers. The original Shocktroops of the NSDAP founded in 1921. It lost its political power to the SS after the 1934 purge. It became responsible for the pre-military training of all able-bodied males in 1939

Sturmbann
An SS or SA formation roughly the size of a battallion

Totenkopfverbände or TV
Death's Heads units. Originally made up of volunteers from the
Allgemeine SS. Employed as concentration guards. Formed the nucleus
of the first field formations of the Waffen-SS

Verfügungstruppe
The original militarised formations of the SS renamed Waffen SS in
939

Vernichtungslager
An extermination camp

Vertrauensmann
An intelligence agent or informer

Volksbund fur das Deutschtum im Ausland
The league for Germans abroad. A pre Nazi organization taken over by
he Party in 1930

Volkskartei
The national register kept by the administrative police

Wachverbände
Original SS concentration camp guards, later became the SS Totenkopfverbande

Waffen SS
The militarized formations of the SS. Originally composed of the
Verfugunsgstruppe and the Totenkopfverbande. Combined non
German SS units after 1940

Wehrmacht
The armed forces

Wehrwirtschaft
War or military economy

Wirtschafts-und Verwaltungshauptamt
The SS economic and administrative office which controlled the
economic enterprise of the SS and administered the concentration
camps. It was run by Oswald Pohl

Zellenleiter
Cell leader. A NSPAD official responsible for about four blocks of
households

Zollgrenzdienst
The border customs service

Editor-in-Chief: Barrie Pitt
Art Director: Sarah Kingham
Editor: David Mason
Cover/Design Consultant: Denis Piper
Design: Michael Fry
Captions: Laurie Milner

The co-operation and help of the following are gratefully acknowledged: the staff of the IWM, London; Mark Dinely of the Bapty Collection; Charles Lewis and George Henderson.